# GRAPHIC NONFICTION

# HERNÁN CORTÉS

## THE LIFE OF A SPANISH CONQUISTADOR

*by*
**DAVID WEST & JACKIE GAFF**

*illustrated by*
**JIM ELDRIDGE**

The Rosen Publishing Group, Inc., New York

Published in 2005 by The Rosen Publishing Group, Inc.
29 East 21st Street, New York, NY 10010

**First edition, 2005**

Designed and produced by
David West Books

*Editor:* Gail Bushnell
*Photo Research:* Carlotta Cooper

Photo credits:
Page 5 (top) – (G. Tortoli) Ancient Art & Architecture Collection Ltd.
Pages 5 (bottom), 6 (bottom), 7 (bottom), 44 (bottom), 45 – Mary Evans Picture Library
Pages 6 (top), 7 (top), 44 (top) – The Culture Archive Picture Library

Library of Congress Cataloging-in-Publication Data

West, David, 1956–
    Hernán Cortés : the life of a Spanish conquistador/by David West and Jackie Gaff—
    1st ed.
    p. cm. — (Graphic nonfiction)
    Includes index.
    ISBN 1-4042-0244-7 (lib. bdg.)
    1. Cortés, Hernán, 1485–1547—Juvenile literature. 2. Mexico—History—Conquest,
    1519–1540—Juvenile literature. 3. Conquerors—Mexico—Biography—Juvenile
    literature. 4. Governors—Mexico—Biography—Juvenile literature. I. Gaff, Jackie. II.
    Title. III. Series.

    F1230.C385W47 2005
    972'.02'092—dc22

                                                                    2004005938

Manufactured in U.S.A.

# CONTENTS

## WHO'S WHO

**Hernán Cortés** (1485–1547) Spanish conquistador, whose 1519 expedition led to the conquest of the Aztec Empire in 1521. His name is also spelled Hernando Cortéz.

**Montezuma, or Moctezuma, II** (1466–1520) Aztec emperor who ruled from 1502 until his death during the Spanish conquest.

**Geronimo de Aguilar** (c. 1489–1531) Spaniard who learned the language of the Maya after being shipwrecked on the Yucatan Peninsula in 1511. He joined Cortés's expedition as an interpreter in 1519.

**La Malinche** (*dates unknown*) A native Indian Mexica woman who spoke the languages of the Maya and Aztecs. She served with de Aguilar as an interpreter for the 1519 expedition. She became Cortés's companion and bore his son, Martin.

**Diego Velázquez** (1465–1524) Spanish conquistador who conquered Cuba in 1511. He founded a colony there and became its first governor.

**Pedro de Alvarado** (c. 1485–1541) Spanish conquistador who was one of Cortés's most trusted deputies on the 1519 expedition.

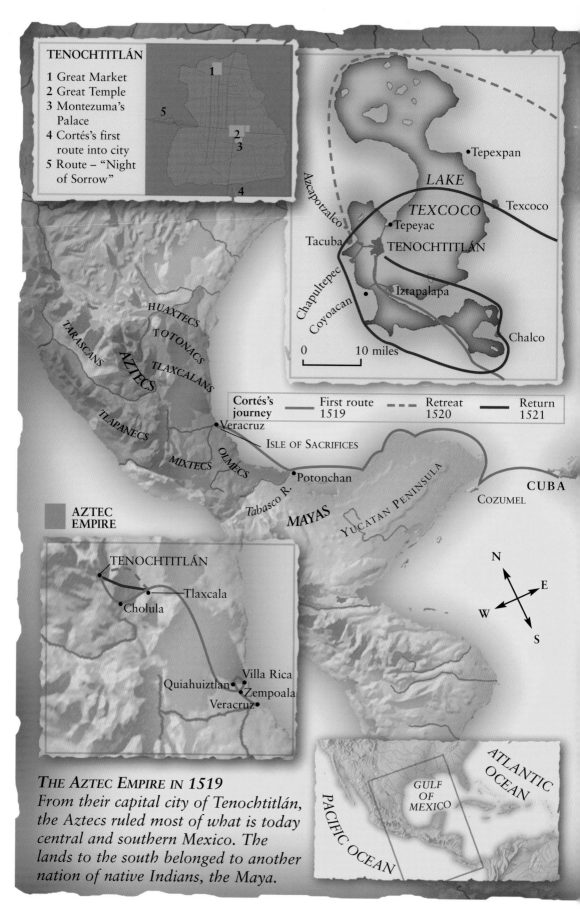

TENOCHTITLÁN

1 Great Market
2 Great Temple
3 Montezuma's Palace
4 Cortés's first route into city
5 Route – "Night of Sorrow"

Tepexpan

LAKE

TEXCOCO

Texcoco

Azcapotzalco

Tepeyac

Tacuba

TENOCHTITLÁN

Chapultepec

Coyoacan

Iztapalapa

Chalco

0      10 miles

HUAXTECS

TOTONACS

TARASCANS

AZTECS

TLAXCALANS

TLAPANECS

MIXTECS   OLMECS

Veracruz

ISLE OF SACRIFICES

Potonchan

Tabasco R.   MAYAS

YUCATAN PENINSULA

COZUMEL

CUBA

Cortés's journey | First route 1519 | --- Retreat 1520 | Return 1521

AZTEC EMPIRE

TENOCHTITLÁN

Tlaxcala

Cholula

Villa Rica

Quiahuiztlan

Zempoala

Veracruz

N
E
W
S

ATLANTIC OCEAN

GULF OF MEXICO

PACIFIC OCEAN

## THE AZTEC EMPIRE IN 1519
*From their capital city of Tenochtitlán, the Aztecs ruled most of what is today central and southern Mexico. The lands to the south belonged to another nation of native Indians, the Maya.*

# THE NEW WORLD

*O*n October 12, 1492, the explorer *Christopher Columbus became the first European to set foot in the region we now call the West Indies. He landed on an island that he named San Salvador. One of his first requests to the natives was for gold.*

### EXPLORERS AND SETTLERS

One of the aims of Columbus's exploration was to discover riches for himself and for King Ferdinand and Queen Isabella of Spain, who had funded his voyage. When Columbus returned with gold, Ferdinand and Isabella claimed the new lands for Spain. Soon, Europe was calling the region the New World. Other explorers flocked there, along with settlers who founded colonies. For many years, Europeans knew little about the mainland to the west of the Indies. They landed in some parts of the mainland, including the Yucatan Peninsula, but they believed they were exploring more islands. The most famous expedition to the mainland was led by Hernán Cortés in 1519.

*EUROPE'S GREED FOR GOLD*
*In Europe, gold was prized as the most valuable form of money. Gold was not used as money in the Americas. Instead it was valued for its beauty.*

### HERNÁN CORTÉS

The son of a poor but noble family, Cortés was born in the Spanish town of Medellin in 1485. He studied law for a while as a young man, but soon decided that being a soldier would be a quicker route to fame and fortune. He was 19 when he arrived in the West Indies in 1504. Five years later, he settled in the Spanish colony on the island of Cuba. Here, Cortés made a good impression on the governor by showing his skill fighting the natives. He was also very ambitious and made his fortune by finding gold on his land. Cortés was known as a gambler and a ladies' man – behavior that got him into fights and even prison!

*SPREADING THE WORD*
*As Christians, the Europeans believed in a single, all-powerful God. The natives of the New World had many gods. Priests traveled with the expeditions to convert the natives to the Christian faith – by force if necessary.*

# WORLDS AT WAR

*C*ortés was a soldier by training and a fortune hunter by nature. When rumors reached Cuba of a mysterious native civilization where gold was as common as dust, he grabbed the chance to be the first to find the riches.

*BATTLE TACTICS*
*Aztec warriors wore amazing costumes that stood for their rank. The more enemies they captured, the higher their rank.*

### THE CONQUERORS

Cortés's 1519 expedition took him into the lands of the Aztecs, in what is today central and southern Mexico. Within three years, his hunt for gold led to the deaths of tens of thousands of Aztecs and the destruction of the Aztec Empire. Cortés and his fellow soldiers were more interested in conquest than exploration. That is why they are known as conquistadors, from the Spanish word for "conquerors."

### THE AZTEC EMPIRE

The Aztec Empire was made up of many towns and cities, but the largest was the Aztec capital city of Tenochtitlán. At the time of Cortés's invasion, Tenochtitlán was home to as many as 250,000 people. No Spanish city of the period was as big. Tenochtitlán was built on islands in Lake Texcoco and, like the Italian city of Venice, was crisscrossed by canals and streets.

### HUMAN SACRIFICE

*Death by sacrifice was a holy act for the Aztecs. Their priests killed captives by cutting out their hearts. This shocked the Spaniards, but the Aztecs were just as horrified by the Europeans, who killed people in battle or burned them at the stake.*

## ENEMIES AND ALLIES

The Aztecs had built their huge empire by conquering other native peoples. Aztec nobles were sent to rule the conquered towns and cities. The people were forced to make tribute payments. These were taxes paid in goods, because the Aztecs had no money system. The tribute payments were very unpopular, and many of the conquered towns and cities offered to help Cortés fight the Aztecs. When Cortés left Cuba in February 1519, his army was made up of about 600 men. The Aztecs had tens of thousands of warriors. Cortés would not have been able to defeat them without the support of the allies he made in the conquered towns and cities.

*EVERY PICTURE TELLS A STORY*
*The Aztecs did not have an alphabet. Instead, they wrote in picture-symbols called glyphs. Some of their books survived the fall of their empire. The books tell us much about the Aztecs' way of life and how they ruled their lands.*

## THE WINNING EDGE

European weapons gave Cortés another key advantage. The conquistadors were armed with metal swords, guns, and cannons. Aztec warriors fought with wooden swords, spears, and arrows edged with a hard glass called obsidian. The Aztecs' weapons were sharp, but the Europeans' weapons were far more deadly. There were also vast differences in the two nations' battle tactics. The Spaniards fought to kill, and they did not take prisoners. The Aztecs did not fight to kill in battle. Instead, they fought to capture prisoners to sacrifice to their gods. The Aztecs honored human sacrifice, believing that after death the victim won life with the gods.

*PROTECTIVE MEASURES*
*Few conquistadors had full suits of metal armor, but even a breastplate offered some protection against Aztec weapons. Aztec warriors only had wooden shields and padded cotton armor to protect themselves.*

CORTÉS IS ONE OF THE RICHEST MEN IN CUBA. HE MADE A FORTUNE BY FINDING GOLD THERE. HE IS ALSO HIGH UP IN THE GOVERNMENT AND HAS THE EAR OF GOVERNOR VELÁZQUEZ – OR USED TO!

"WHEN RUMORS REACHED VELÁZQUEZ OF THE WEALTH TO BE FOUND IN THE YUCATAN PENINSULA, HE DECIDED TO SEND AN EXPEDITION TO TRADE WITH THE NATIVES. CORTÉS WAS TOLD HE COULD LEAD IT IF HE PAID MOST OF THE COSTS.

CORTÉS PUT TOGETHER A FLEET OF 11 SHIPS, ALONG WITH THE SMALL ARMY YOU SEE HERE. IT COST HIM A FORTUNE!

NOW WHY WOULD HE SPEND THAT KIND OF MONEY UNLESS HE THOUGHT HE COULD MAKE MORE?

VELÁZQUEZ HAD SECOND THOUGHTS AND SENT ORDERS TAKING THE COMMAND AWAY FROM CORTÉS.

CORTÉS'S BROTHER-IN-LAW **KILLED** THE MESSENGER...

...THEN TOOK THE ORDERS TO CORTÉS **HIMSELF.**

VELÁZQUEZ RUSHED TO THE DOCKS, ONLY TO FIND THAT CORTÉS WAS **ALREADY** ROWING OUT TO HIS SHIP."

BUT NOTHING WAS GOING TO STOP CORTÉS. HE TOLD HIS FLEET TO SET SAIL.

SO YOU SEE, ALL OF US WHO SAILED WITH HIM ARE REBELS IN A WAY!

A FEW DAYS AFTER MY TALK WITH THE CONQUISTADORA, OUR EXPEDITION ROUNDED THE TIP OF THE YUCATAN. SOON WE REACHED THE MOUTH OF THE TABASCO RIVER.

WE ANCHORED A SHORT WAY UPRIVER, NEAR A TOWN CALLED POTONCHAN. THE NATIVES GAVE US FOOD AND A GOLD MASK, BUT THEY SEEMED ON EDGE.

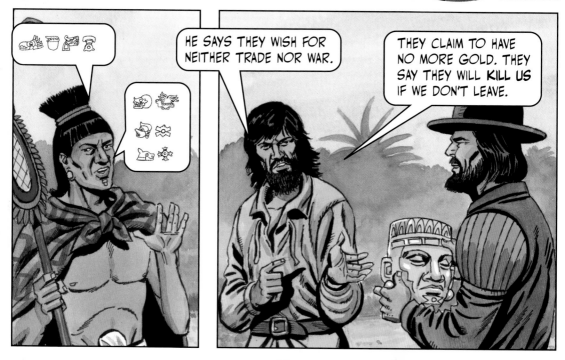

HE SAYS THEY WISH FOR NEITHER TRADE NOR WAR.

THEY CLAIM TO HAVE NO MORE GOLD. THEY SAY THEY WILL **KILL US** IF WE DON'T LEAVE.

DURING THE NEXT FEW DAYS, IT BECAME CLEAR THAT THE NATIVES WERE PREPARING TO CARRY OUT THEIR THREAT.

WHEN THEY DID ATTACK, WE WERE READY...

A FEW OF OUR MEN WERE WOUNDED, BUT MANY OF THE NATIVES WERE KILLED.

THE NATIVES HAD NEVER SEEN WEAPONS LIKE OURS BEFORE. THEY FLED FROM OUR CROSSBOWS, CANNONS, AND MATCHLOCKS.*

*AN EARLY TYPE OF GUN THAT TOOK A LONG TIME TO LOAD. THEY MADE A GREAT DEAL OF NOISE AND SMOKE, WHICH MUST HAVE TERRIFIED THE NATIVES.

THE DEFEATED NATIVES OF POTONCHAN **SHOWERED US** WITH GIFTS, INCLUDING WOMEN TO SERVE AND COOK FOR US.

GUNPOWDER GIVES ME THE POWER TO STRIKE FEAR INTO THE NATIVES' HEARTS. BUT I NEED ALSO TO READ THEIR MINDS.

CORTÉS HAD LEARNED THAT THE GOLD HE DESIRED SO MUCH CAME FROM FAR INLAND, FROM THE GREAT EMPIRE OF THE AZTEC PEOPLE. THE AZTECS SPOKE NAHUATL, A LANGUAGE I COULD NOT HELP HIM WITH. BUT FORTUNE WAS SMILING ON CORTÉS...

GERONIMO, THAT WOMAN, – HER WORDS SOUND STRANGE.

YOU ARE RIGHT, SIR. I DO NOT UNDERSTAND THEM.

ASK HER WHERE SHE IS FROM.

NOW I HAVE THE MEANS TO TALK WITH THE AZTECS!

SHE UNDERSTANDS MAYAN AND SAYS HER NAME IS MALINCHE. HER FATHER WAS LORD OF AN AZTEC TOWN, BUT SHE WAS SOLD INTO SLAVERY AFTER HIS DEATH.

SO SHE ALSO **SPEAKS NAHUATL!**

MALINCHE – THAT'S A BEAUTIFUL NAME.

FROM THAT DAY ON, CORTÉS AND LA MALINCHE WERE INSEPARABLE. SHE WAS TO SERVE AS HIS EARS AND MOUTH WHEN IT CAME TO DEALING WITH THE AZTECS.*

*MALINCHE'S OWN PEOPLE CAME TO SEE HER AS A TRAITOR. IN MEXICO EVEN TODAY, A **MALINCHISTA** IS A PERSON WHO PREFERS SOMETHING FOREIGN.

OUR FLEET SET SAIL AGAIN. ON APRIL 20, WE REACHED A SMALL ISLAND. THE CONQUISTADORS CALLED IT THE **ISLE OF SACRIFICES.**

THAT'S AN EERIE NAME FOR SUCH A BEAUTIFUL PLACE.

THESE NATIVES SEEM PLEASED TO SEE US – BUT NOT AS FUTURE SACRIFICES, I HOPE.

YES, IT WAS NAMED LAST YEAR BY THE TRADING EXPEDITION LED BY VELÁZQUEZ'S NEPHEW, JUAN DE GRIJALVA. IT'S ONE OF THE PLACES WHERE THE AZTECS CARRY OUT HUMAN SACRIFICE. IT'S LITTERED WITH BONES.

NO, THEY ARE TOTONACS AND THEY ARE RULED BY THE AZTECS. THE TOTONACS WANT THEIR FREEDOM, AND THEY PROBABLY HOPE WE'LL HELP THEM.

15

WE SET UP CAMP AMONG THE SAND DUNES ON THE COAST.* THE AZTECS SOON HEARD OF OUR ARRIVAL. WITHIN TWO DAYS, A COLUMN OF PORTERS REACHED US, BEARING GIFTS FROM THE AZTEC EMPEROR, MONTEZUMA II.

*THE CITY OF VERACRUZ TODAY STANDS ON THE SITE.

I REMEMBER THE NEXT DAY WAS EASTER SUNDAY...

MONTEZUMA HAS HEARD OF YOUR BATTLE WITH THE PEOPLE OF POTONCHAN. HE HAS SENT HIS AMBASSADOR, TEUDILE, TO GREET YOU.

CORTÉS'S FIRST SURPRISE WAS TEUDILE'S SPLENDID PARROT-FEATHER CLOAK. HIS SECOND WAS THE AZTEC'S GREETING...

WHAT THE – ?

HE'S EATING DIRT!

16

NEXT IT WAS TEUDILE'S TURN TO LOOK AMAZED, AS WE BEGAN OUR EASTER PRAYER SERVICE.

CORTÉS AND TEUDILE THEN SAT DOWN TO EAT, WHILE MALINCHE AND I TRANSLATED.

WHERE IS YOUR RULER? WE WOULD LIKE TO MEET HIM.

TEUDILE SAYS HE WILL CARRY YOUR WORDS TO THE EMPEROR.

TEUDILE THEN PRESENTED CORTÉS WITH MORE GIFTS, MANY MADE OF GOLD.

OUR GIFTS SEEMED POOR IN COMPARISON. THE AZTECS SEEMED TO THINK THEY WERE WORTHLESS.

BUT CORTÉS KNEW HOW TO IMPRESS THE AZTECS. THEY FELL DOWN IN FEAR WHEN WE SHOWED OFF OUR FIREPOWER...

THIS WILL SEND ITS OWN MESSAGE TO MONTEZUMA!

BEFORE HE RETURNED HOME, TEUDILE ASKED CORTÉS WHY HE WANTED GOLD SO MUCH...

TELL HIM MY MEN SUFFER FROM A DISEASE OF THE HEART THAT CAN ONLY BE CURED BY GOLD.

LATER I LEARNED OF TEUDILE'S RETURN HOME AND OF THE
MESSENGERS WHO SPED BEFORE HIM CARRYING THE NEWS...

...PAST COLUMNS OF MEN CARRYING TRIBUTE
PAYMENTS OF FOOD, CLOTH, AND CAPTIVES...

...PAST THATCH-ROOFED TOWNS WHERE CRAFTSMEN
WORKED GOLD, JEWELS, AND FEATHERS...

...AND THROUGH RICH FARMLANDS WHERE
MAIZE AND VEGETABLES ARE GROWN.

UNTIL AT LAST THEY CAME DOWN INTO THE VALLEY OF LAKE TEXCOCO AND THE
AZTECS' GREAT ISLAND CITY OF TENOCHTITLÁN. IT WAS HOME TO MORE THAN
250,000 PEOPLE — FARMERS, CRAFTSMEN, TRADERS, AND WARRIORS.

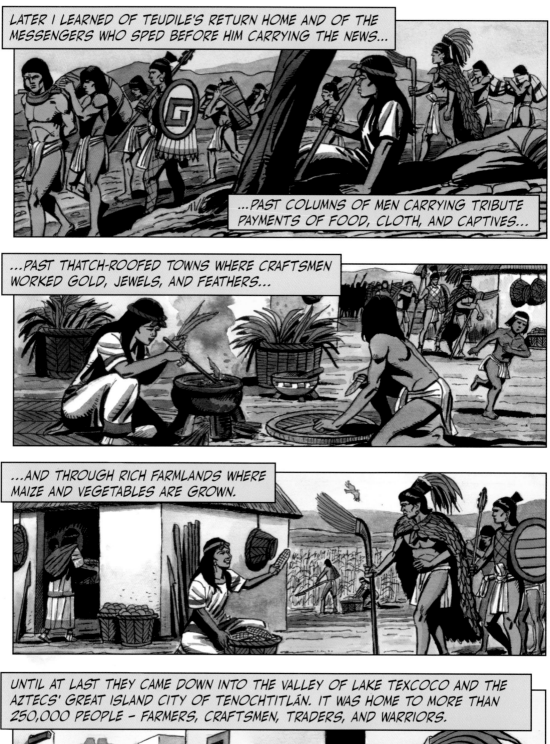

IN THE GREAT TEMPLE, MONTEZUMA SAT ON A MAT WHILE THE PRIESTS MOVED ABOUT AMID THE SMELL OF INCENSE AND DRIED BLOOD.

TLATOANI* – MESSENGERS BRING NEWS AT LAST.

THEY MUST BE PURIFIED.

*TLATOANI IS THE TITLE THE AZTECS GAVE THEIR RULER. IT MEANS "GREAT SPEAKER."

AT THE TOP OF THE GREAT TEMPLE, THE AZTEC PRIESTS PREPARED A CAPTIVE FOR SACRIFICE. THEY HELD HIM OVER A STONE ALTAR. THEN A KNIFE FLASHED DOWN THROUGH THE AIR...

...TO RIP HIS HEART FROM HIS BODY!

THE BLOOD WAS SPRINKLED OVER THE MESSENGERS TO PURIFY THEM.

THE MESSENGERS TOLD OF THEIR ENCOUNTERS WITH THE SPANIARDS...

THEY COVER ALL THEIR BODIES WITH CLOTHES, EXCEPT FOR THEIR FACES.

MOST HAVE BEARDS, AND THEIR BATTLE CLOTHES ARE MADE OF IRON.

THEIR WEAPONS ARE IRON, TOO, AND **SPURT FIRE!**

AZTEC ARTISTS HAD RECORDED EVERYTHING THE STRANGERS WORE AND DID. *EVERY DETAIL* WAS ANALYZED, EVEN DOWN TO WHAT THE STRANGERS ATE.

MONTEZUMA HAD TO DECIDE WHAT TO DO ABOUT THE STRANGERS. BUT HE FOUND IT ALMOST IMPOSSIBLE TO UNDERSTAND THEIR BEHAVIOR...

HUMAN SACRIFICE SICKENS THEM. THE GOD QUETZALCOATL IS ALSO AGAINST IT.

QUETZALCOATL, THE FEATHERED SERPENT, WHO LONG AGO HAD VANISHED ACROSS THE SEA TOWARD THE EAST.

QUETZALCOATL, THE WARRIOR OF THE DAWN, WHO PROMISED TO RETURN FROM THE PLACE WHERE THE SUN RISES.

21

MEANWHILE, WE WERE WAITING FOR MONTEZUMA'S NEXT MOVE. CORTÉS USED THE TIME TO SOLVE HIS PROBLEM WITH GOVERNOR VELÁZQUEZ BACK IN CUBA.

I CANNOT RETURN TO CUBA. THEY'LL HANG ME!

CORTÉS KNEW A LOT ABOUT THE LAW. HIS FIRST MOVE WAS TO SET UP A LOCAL SPANISH GOVERNMENT. HE CALLED IT THE TOWN COUNCIL OF VILLA RICA DE VERA CRUZ.*

IT WILL BE THE FIRST **LEGAL** SPANISH AUTHORITY IN MAINLAND AMERICA.

*A TOWN WAS BUILT AND NAMED VILLA RICA. IT WAS THE FIRST SPANISH SETTLEMENT ON THE AMERICAN MAINLAND.

NEXT, HE QUIT THE POST OF EXPEDITION LEADER GIVEN TO HIM BY VELÁZQUEZ.

FINALLY, HE GOT HIS NEW AUTHORITY, THE TOWN COUNCIL, TO MAKE HIM EXPEDITION LEADER INSTEAD.

NOW, THE ONLY LEGAL AUTHORITY ABOVE ME IS THE SPANISH CROWN.

IF I CONQUER THESE LANDS AND SET UP THE CHRISTIAN FAITH HERE, THE KING WILL SURELY REWARD ME.

BUT FIRST, I NEED SOME ALLIES.

SOON AFTER, WORD CAME FROM THE TOTONAC KING, INVITING US TO VISIT HIS CAPITAL CITY, ZEMPOALA. OUR FLEET SAILED UP THE COAST, CLOSER TO ZEMPOALA. IT ANCHORED IN A NEARBY BAY.

CORTÉS MADE GOOD USE OF HIS TIME WITH THE TOTONACS. WE TRAINED THREE NATIVE PRIESTS IN THE CHRISTIAN FAITH.

WE ALSO LEARNED OF THE MANY OTHER KINGDOMS RULED BY THE AZTECS.

THE TLAXCALANS LIVE FARTHER INLAND. THEY ARE OLD ENEMIES OF THE AZTECS.

HMMM — USEFUL ALLIES, PERHAPS?

WHILE WE WERE IN ZEMPOALA, THE AZTECS' TRIBUTE COLLECTORS VISITED A NEARBY TOTONAC TOWN.

CORTÉS TALKED THE TOTONACS INTO IMPRISONING THE AZTECS.

BUT LATER THAT NIGHT, HE HAD THE AZTECS SECRETLY RELEASED...

TELL HIM TO TELL MONTEZUMA THAT CORTÉS IS A FRIEND, NOT A FOE.

THE TOTONACS WERE WORRIED WHEN THEY LEARNED THE AZTECS WERE FREE...

THEY FEAR THE REVENGE OF MONTEZUMA.

TELL HIM CORTÉS IS THEIR FRIEND AND WILL PROTECT THEM.

23

NOT EVERYONE WAS TAKEN IN BY CORTÉS. A FEW OF OUR MEN WERE STILL LOYAL TO VELÁZQUEZ. THEY SAW THROUGH CORTÉS'S TRICKS.

GET WORD TO OUR FRIENDS. WE'LL TAKE A BOAT TONIGHT AND SAIL BACK TO CUBA.

VELÁZQUEZ'S ORDERS WERE TO EXPLORE AND TRADE. CORTÉS ONLY WANTS CONQUEST AND GOLD.

BUT CORTÉS HAD EARS EVERYWHERE...

WHAT THE – ?

HAVE MERCY, LORD. I WILL NOT TRY TO ESCAPE AGAIN.

CUT OFF HIS FEET!

LÓPEZ! TAKE EVERYTHING WE NEED FROM OUR SHIPS.

THEN SINK THEM.

THE ONLY WAY TO GO NOW WAS INLAND. CORTÉS WAS RISKING EVERYTHING ON MAKING THE TLAXCALANS OUR ALLIES.

WE LEFT THE COAST AND HEADED UP INTO THE MOUNTAINS.

IT BECAME COLDER AND COLDER AS WE CLIMBED PAST SNOW-CAPPED MOUNTAIN PEAKS.

AFTER MANY DAYS, WE REACHED THE LANDS OF THE TLAXCALANS. BUT THEY DID **NOT** WELCOME US.

INSTEAD, THEY ATTACKED US BY THE THOUSANDS.

SOON WE WERE FORCED BACK TO A SETTLEMENT ON A SMALL HILL. WE WERE SURROUNDED BY THE ENEMY, BUT THEY COULD NOT BREAK OUR RANKS.

WE MANAGED TO HOLD OUT FOR TWO WEEKS.

IN THE END, THE TLAXCALANS REALIZED THEY COULD NOT BEAT US. THEY MADE PEACE WITH US AND AGREED TO JOIN US AS ALLIES IN FIGHTING THE AZTECS.

WE JOURNEYED ON, OUR NUMBERS SWOLLEN BY THOUSANDS OF TLAXCALAN WARRIORS. SOON WE REACHED THE CAPITAL CITY OF THE CHOLULAN PEOPLE.

THE CITY IS **MAGNIFICENT.**

THE TLAXCALANS HATED THE CHOLULANS AND WANTED CORTÉS TO ATTACK THEM.

THEY SAY THE CHOLULANS PLAN TO AMBUSH YOU INSIDE THEIR CITY AND KILL YOU ALL.

THEN WE WILL SPRING A TRAP OF OUR OWN.

THE CHOLULAN LEADERS AND THEIR WARRIORS GATHERED TO MEET CORTÉS IN THE GREAT SQUARE BESIDE THEIR TEMPLE TO THE GOD QUETZALCOATL...

...OVER 3,000 UNARMED CHOLULANS WERE KILLED.

CORTÉS WASTED NO TIME BEFORE MOVING ON TO TENOCHTITLÁN, THE AZTEC CAPITAL...

NEWS OF THE CHOLULAN SLAYINGS SPREAD QUICKLY. PEOPLE WERE TERRIFIED EVERYWHERE WE WENT.

BEFORE WE LEFT THE MOUNTAINS, WE AGAIN MET WITH MESSENGERS FROM MONTEZUMA. THEY BROUGHT US MORE GIFTS OF GOLD.

THEY ARE LIKE MONKEYS WITH FRUIT.

GOLD!

GOLD!

HOW MUCH **MORE** DO THEY HAVE?

FINALLY, WE REACHED THE VALLEY OF LAKE TEXCOCO. THERE, BEFORE US LAY TENOCHTITLÁN, GLIMMERING LIKE A GOLDEN JEWEL SET IN JADE-GREEN WATER.

CORTÉS SENT MESSENGERS TO THE RULERS OF THE LAKESIDE TOWNS.

GOOD NEWS, LORD. NONE OF THE LAKESIDE TOWNS WILL RESIST US.

SO ALL WE HAVE TO DEAL WITH ARE THE AZTECS THEMSELVES.

THE AZTECS' GRIP OVER THEIR EMPIRE WAS WEAK. THE CONQUERED TOWNS WERE UNHAPPY WITH AZTEC RULE AND THE TRIBUTE PAYMENTS DEMANDED BY THEIR AZTEC MASTERS. THE TOWNS HOPED CORTÉS WOULD SET THEM FREE.

IT IS THE MOST BEAUTIFUL CITY IN THE WORLD!

THE MAIN CAUSEWAY INTO THE AZTECS' CAPITAL CITY LAY BEFORE US.

ON NOVEMBER 8, 1519, WE MARCHED ACROSS THE CAUSEWAY INTO TENOCHTITLÁN.

WE WERE WATCHED BY THOUSANDS OF CURIOUS AZTECS – IN CANOES, ON ROOFTOPS, AND IN THE STREETS.

THERE WERE BARELY 400 OF US SPANIARDS. OUR HORSEMEN LED THE WAY, TRYING TO JUDGE THE CROWD'S MOOD. WOULD THE AZTECS TURN ON US?

BEFORE WE CROSSED THE FINAL BRIDGE INTO THE CITY, WE HAD TO PASS THROUGH A FORTLIKE BUILDING.

SOON, WE MET WITH A SPLENDIDLY DRESSED AZTEC. HE WAS AT THE HEAD OF A LONG COLUMN OF MEN...

ASK IF HE IS MONTEZUMA.

HE SAYS HE IS.

WE WERE GIVEN A GRAND BUILDING WITH ITS OWN COURTYARD AS OUR COMPOUND. WE FIRED OUR GUNS TO SHOW THE AZTECS OUR POWER.

MONTEZUMA SPOKE WORDS OF WELCOME. HE URGED US TO REST AFTER OUR LONG JOURNEY.

IN THE DAYS THAT FOLLOWED, I WAS OFTEN WITH CORTÉS AND LA MALINCHE. ONCE WE WERE EVEN ALLOWED TO CLIMB WITH MONTEZUMA TO THE TOP OF HIS GREAT TEMPLE.

ASK HIM IF WE CAN PLACE A CHRISTIAN ALTAR HERE.

THEY HOLD THEIR OWN WAYS TO BE GOOD. HE SAYS TO TALK NO MORE TO HIM ABOUT IT.

THE VIEW FROM THE TOP SHOWED OFF THE CITY IN ALL ITS SPLENDOR.

WE WERE FORTUNATE ENOUGH TO BE ABLE TO VISIT MANY OF THE SITES OF TENOCHTITLÁN. MY FAVORITE WAS THE CITY'S VAST MARKET...

AS MANY AS 60,000 PEOPLE WERE THERE ON MARKET DAY, BUYING AND SELLING EVERYTHING UNDER THE SUN. THERE WERE FLOWERS, FOOD, CLOTHES, AND HOUSEHOLD GOODS, AS WELL AS SPLENDID CRAFTWORK AND JEWELRY.

30

WE ALSO WITNESSED A MOST ENTERTAINING SPORT, CALLED TLACHTLI. THE GAME WAS HELD IN A GREAT I-SHAPED STADIUM. THE PLAYERS ATTEMPTED TO GET A BALL THROUGH A STONE CIRCLE IN ONE OF THE WALLS.

CORTÉS MADE HIS MOVE EIGHT DAYS AFTER OUR ARRIVAL. HE CAPTURED MONTEZUMA AND HELD HIM PRISONER. OVER THE NEXT FEW WEEKS, CORTÉS TRIED TO RULE THE AZTECS THROUGH MONTEZUMA.

EARLY IN 1520, CORTÉS MADE MONTEZUMA CALL HIS CHIEF NOBLES TO A SPECIAL MEETING. CORTÉS THEN **FORCED** THE AZTECS TO AGREE TO BE RULED BY THE SPANISH KING. MEMBERS OF THE AZTECS' FAMILIES WERE TAKEN HOSTAGE. THIS WAS DONE TO MAKE SURE THE NOBLES KEPT THEIR WORD.

MONTEZUMA WAS ALSO FORCED TO ALLOW US TO SET UP CHRISTIAN SHRINES ON HIS GREAT TEMPLE.

31

EVERYTHING SEEMED TO BE GOING CORTÉS'S WAY. BUT IN EARLY APRIL, BAD NEWS ARRIVED FROM THE COAST...

VELÁZQUEZ HAD SENT AN EXPEDITION UNDER PANFILO DE NARVAEZ TO ARREST CORTÉS.

CORTÉS WAS DETERMINED TO WIN HIS TRY FOR POWER. HE CALLED FOR ONE OF HIS MOST TRUSTED ASSISTANTS, PEDRO DE ALVARADO.

PEDRO, I'M LEAVING YOU HERE WITH 100 MEN TO GUARD MONTEZUMA AND THE HOSTAGES.

CORTÉS TOOK THE REST OF US BACK TO THE COAST.

HE WAS LEADING US TO BATTLE AGAINST OUR OWN COUNTRYMEN.

ON A RAINY NIGHT, WE ATTACKED...

NARVAEZ WAS WOUNDED ALMOST IMMEDIATELY.

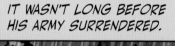

AARGH!

IT WASN'T LONG BEFORE HIS ARMY SURRENDERED.

CORTÉS TALKED NARVAEZ'S MEN INTO JOINING US. HE PROMISED THEM GOLD AS A REWARD. WE RETURNED TO TENOCHTITLÁN WITH ABOUT 1,000 MORE SOLDIERS.

33

SOON WE LEARNED THAT THE AZTECS HAD CHOSEN A NEW RULER, CALLED *CUITLAHUAC*. WE WERE TRAPPED INSIDE THE CITY. THE AZTECS HAD TORN UP THE BRIDGES OVER THE CAUSEWAYS TO STOP US FROM LEAVING.

WE HAD TO BREAK FREE. CORTÉS PLANNED A DARING ESCAPE FOR THE NIGHT OF JULY 1.

OUR CARPENTER, MARTIN LÓPEZ, MADE A BRIDGE FROM ROOF BEAMS. MOST OF OUR GOLD WAS BOXED UP AND LOADED ONTO OUR HORSES. THE REST WAS CARRIED BY OUR MEN. WE SET OFF AT MIDNIGHT. A LIGHT RAIN WAS FALLING.

WE WERE ON THE CAUSEWAY WHEN WE WERE SPOTTED. OUR BRIDGE WAS BEHIND US. ANOTHER GAP LAY AHEAD.

WITHIN MINUTES, WE WERE SURROUNDED BY AZTEC WARRIORS IN THEIR CANOES. AS OUR MEN AT THE BACK RUSHED ON IN PANIC, THEIR COMRADES AT THE FRONT WERE FORCED INTO THE WATER...

THEY ARE RUNNING AWAY! COME QUICK!

HUNDREDS OF OUR MEN WERE DEAD. WE CALLED IT THE NIGHT OF SORROW. WE SURVIVORS RETREATED TOWARD TLAXCALA, OUR ALLIES' CAPITAL CITY.

AN ARMY OF AZTEC WARRIORS RAPIDLY FOLLOWED US.

THEY CAUGHT UP WITH US A FEW DAYS LATER, NEAR THE TOWN OF OTUMBA.

CLOSE RANKS!

EVEN THOUGH OUR POSITION SEEMED HOPELESS, CORTÉS DID NOT LOSE HIS NERVE.

OUR MEN FOUGHT BACK BRAVELY, BUT WE WERE SURROUNDED BY THOUSANDS OF AZTEC WARRIORS.

GLEURGH!

LOOK! THE AZTEC GENERALS ARE SIGNALING THEIR ATTACKS FROM THAT HILL.

CORTÉS LED THE CHARGE ON THE SIGNAL HILL...

YAARRRGH!

OOMPH!

THIS BOLD MOVE WON US ENOUGH TIME TO ESCAPE INTO THE LANDS OF OUR ALLIES, THE TLAXCALANS.

MEANWHILE, TENOCHTITLÁN WAS UNDER ATTACK FROM AN INVISIBLE ENEMY. THE DEADLY DISEASE SMALLPOX WAS UNKNOWN IN THE AMERICAS UNTIL WE EUROPEANS ARRIVED. NOW IT WAS KILLING THOUSANDS OF NATIVES. IT EVEN TOOK THE LIFE OF THE NEW EMPEROR, CUITLAHUAC.

IN TLAXCALA, CORTÉS WAS PLOTTING TO RECAPTURE TENOCHTITLÁN. THIS TIME HE PLANNED TO USE SHIPS TO TAKE THE CAUSEWAYS.

LÓPEZ, I NEED SHIPS.

WE CAN MAKE THEM HERE AND THEN TAKE THEM APART FOR TRANSPORTATION.

MARTIN LÓPEZ TOOK CHARGE OF BUILDING 13 SHIPS. ONCE TESTED, THEY WERE TAKEN APART SO THAT THEY COULD BE CARRIED TO THE LAKE.

CORTÉS WROTE TO THE KING OF SPAIN AND WON ROYAL SUPPORT FOR THE ATTACK ON TENOCHTITLÁN. MORE SOLDIERS AND SUPPLIES WERE SENT FROM CUBA.

OUR ARMY SET OFF A FEW DAYS AFTER CHRISTMAS, 1520. WE HAD WELL OVER 500 CONQUISTADORS AND AT LEAST 10,000 TLAXCALAN WARRIORS.

WE SET UP BASE AT THE TOWN OF TEXCOCO. CORTÉS PLANNED TO CAPTURE ALL THE LAKESIDE TOWNS BEFORE LAYING SIEGE TO TENOCHTITLÁN.

IF WE CUT OFF THE AZTEC CAPITAL, THE NEW EMPEROR, CUAUHTEMOC, WILL HAVE TO SURRENDER.

GLEURGH!

BUT NOT EVERYTHING WENT SMOOTHLY. IN ONE TOWN, THE NATIVES BROKE THEIR DAMS AND FLOODED THE STREETS.

OUR SHIPBUILDING WENT WELL. IN LATE MAY 1521, OUR FLEET LAUNCHED A MAJOR ATTACK ON TENOCHTITLÁN'S THREE CAUSEWAYS...

KADOOM

AZTEC WARRIORS TOOK TO THE WATER IN HUNDREDS OF CANOES TO FIGHT BACK. BUT THEY STOOD LITTLE CHANCE AGAINST OUR GUNS AND CANNONS.

AFTER DESTROYING THE AZTECS' CANOES, OUR FLEET CAPTURED THE CAUSEWAYS. OUR ARMY POURED INTO TENOCHTITLÁN...

THE AZTECS FOUGHT BACK BRAVELY. THE BATTLE WENT ON FOR WEEKS.

EACH TIME WE CAPTURED AN AREA, THEY DROVE US OUT THE NEXT DAY.

ON ONE OCCASION, CORTÉS AND SOME CONQUISTADORS FOUND THEMSELVES TRAPPED BETWEEN TWO GROUPS OF AZTEC WARRIORS.

AARGH!

NNGH!

THIS WAY, LORD!

MERCY!

ANY AZTECS WHO ATTACKED THE WORK CREWS WERE KILLED OR DRIVEN AWAY.

OUR FLEET KEPT TENOCHTITLÁN UNDER SIEGE. IT CUT OFF ITS SUPPLIES OF FOOD AND FRESH WATER. THE AZTECS WERE STARVING. BUT THEY WOULD NOT GIVE UP.

IT SEEMED AS THOUGH EVERY LAST AZTEC WAS READY TO DIE FIGHTING.

BUT OUR SOLDIERS PRESSED ON, DESTROYING THE CITY AS THEY WENT. SLOWLY, THE AZTECS WERE FORCED BACK. SOON THEY WERE TRAPPED IN THE NORTHERN TIP OF TENOCHTITLÁN. THERE, THEY MADE THEIR LAST STAND.

A TRUMPET RANG OUT AS WE BEGAN THE FINAL BATTLE. IT LASTED FIVE DAYS...

AAARGH!

NO ONE WAS SPARED. OUR CONQUISTADORS THOUGHT THE AZTECS WERE HIDING THEIR GOLD IN THEIR CLOTHES.

HAND OVER YOUR GOLD!

THE CITY WAS IN RUINS. THE SURVIVING AZTECS FLED.

BY THE BATTLE'S END, 40,000 AZTEC MEN, WOMEN, AND CHILDREN LAY DEAD.

IT WAS AUGUST 13, 1521. THE SIEGE HAD LASTED 80 DAYS.

EMPEROR CUAUHTEMOC WAS BROUGHT BEFORE CORTÉS...

HE SAYS HE DID HIS DUTY IN DEFENDING HIS CITY. HE BEGS YOU TO END HIS LIFE.

LATER I HEARD THAT CORTÉS HAD CUAUHTEMOC TORTURED TO FIND OUT WHERE THE AZTECS HAD HIDDEN THEIR GOLD.

WHEN CUAUHTEMOC COULD NO LONGER SPEAK, HE WAS KILLED.

WE FOUND LITTLE GOLD – NOTHING COMPARED TO WHAT WE LOST ON THE NIGHT OF SORROW. CORTÉS SENT NEWS OF HIS VICTORY TO OUR KING, **CHARLES I** OF SPAIN. CHARLES REWARDED CORTÉS WITH HONORS AND LAND. SETTLERS CAME FROM SPAIN AND BEGAN TO BUILD ON THE RUINS OF TENOCHTITLÁN. THEY RENAMED IT **MEXICO CITY.** IN 1522, THEY DECLARED IT THE CAPITAL OF THE COLONY OF NEW SPAIN.

**THE END**

43

# AFTER THE CONQUEST

The Spanish king, Charles I, rewarded Cortés for his role in the Spanish conquest of the Aztec Empire by appointing him the first governor of New Spain in 1522. Six years later, the king gave Cortés the high noble title of marquis of the Oaxaca Valley.

### CORTÉS AND LA MALINCHE

*Little is known about the fate of Cortés's companion, La Malinche. Cortés is thought to have married her off to one of his conquistadors. No one knows what happened to her afterward.*

### SPANISH RULE

As governor, Cortés oversaw the setting up of Spanish rule throughout the new colony. Spanish soldiers backed by native allies were sent to conquer the regions around Tenochtitlán. The conquered lands were divided into huge estates. These were run by Spanish landlords and worked by natives. The Spaniards also worked to convert the natives to Christianity. Aztec temples were destroyed and the statues of Aztec gods were smashed. Christian churches were built and Christian schools were started. Despite these efforts, some of the Aztecs' religious customs lived on. For example, Aztec autumn festivals are still held in the Day of the Dead celebrations in modern Mexico.

### CITIZENS OF NEW SPAIN

*Most of the Spaniards who flocked to New Spain in the sixteenth century were men. A few brought their wives with them. Many Spanish soldiers and settlers had children by native women. The mixed-race people of this new society became known as mestizos.*

GULF OF CALIFORNIA

GULF OF MEXICO

1535

•Tenochtitlán

YUCATAN PENINSULA

1524 – 1526

GUATEMALA  Trujillo •

HONDURAS

### New Adventures

*Cortés's days as a conquistador did not end in 1522. He sent an expedition under Pedro de Alvarado to Guatemala in 1524. In 1525, Cortés led an expedition to Honduras. During the 1530s, he explored the Gulf of California.*

## CORTÉS'S FALL FROM GRACE

In 1528, Cortés began a two-year visit to Spain. His first wife, Catalina, had died in 1522. Many people believed he had strangled her. The charge was investigated by Spanish officials. Cortés was found neither guilty nor innocent. The doubt cast a shadow over his name. Rumors also began to spread that Cortés was planning to rebel against Spanish rule and declare the colony of New Spain independent. He was replaced by a new colonial governor, Antonio de Mendoza.

Cortés returned to the colony a far less popular and powerful man than he had left it. In 1540, he went back to Spain for the last time. He died seven years later, on his estate near the city of Seville.

### Final Years

*Cortés's final years were more about failure than success. In 1541, he lost a large part of his fortune and was shipwrecked while taking part in a Spanish expedition against the north African city of Algiers.*

# GLOSSARY

**ally** A person who supports others.

**ambassador** A person who represents the government or ruler of a nation.

**astrologer** Someone who studies the position of the stars and planets.

**barricade** A barrier to prevent people from getting past a certain point.

**causeway** A raised road built across water.

**conquistadors** Spanish soldiers who conquered Mexico, Central America, and Peru in the sixteenth century.

**empire** A group of countries or states that have the same ruler.

**expedition** A journey which has been organized for a particular reason, such as exploration.

**fleet** A group of warships under one command.

**hostage** Someone who is taken and held prisoner as a way of demanding money or other conditions.

**interpreter** Someone who translates a foreign language.

**launch** To put a boat or ship into the water.

**omen** A sign or warning about something that will happen in the future.

**purify** To make something pure or clean.

**rebel** Someone who fights against the people in charge of something.

**sacrifice** The killing of a person or an animal as an offering to a god.

**shrine** A holy place of worship.

**siege** To surround a place and force its people to surrender.

**smallpox** A disease that causes chills, high fever, and pimples.

**tactics** Plans or methods to achieve a goal.

**traitor** Someone who betrays their friends or country.

**tribute** Goods or money paid by one nation to another in return for protection, or to show that the payer accepts the other nation as its ruler.

# FOR MORE INFORMATION

## ORGANIZATION

Southwest Museum of the American Indian
234 Museum Drive
Los Angeles, CA 90065
(323) 221-2164
Web site: http://www.southwestmuseum.org/museum.html

## FOR FURTHER READING

Barghusen, Joan D. *The Aztecs: End of a Civilization*. Farmington Hills, MI: Gale Group, 2000.

Clare, John D. *Aztec Life*. Hauppauge, NY: Barron's Educational Series, Inc., 2000.

De Angelis, Gina. *Hernan Cortes and the Conquest of Mexico*. New York: Chelsea House Publishers, 1999.

Flowers, Charles. *Cortes and the Conquest of the Aztec Empire in World History*. Berkeley Heights, NJ: Enslow Publishers, 2001.

Heili, Mathilde, and Remi Courgeon. *Montezuma and the Aztecs*. New York: Henry Holt & Company, Inc., 1996.

Jovinelly, Joann, and Jason Netelkos. *The Crafts and Culture of the Aztecs*. New York: Rosen Publishing Group, Inc., 2001.

Pohl, John M. *Aztec Warrior, AD 1325–1521*. Oxford, UK: Osprey Publishing, Ltd., 2001.

# INDEX

## Web Sites

Due to the changing nature of Internet links, the Rosen Publishing Group, Inc., has developed an online list of Web sites related to the subject of this book. This site is updated regularly. Please use this link to access the list:

http://www.rosenlinks.com/gnf/cortes